OH TO PAINT A CAT DREAM

A RAP FANTASY

by Linda Smet
also known as Linda Samet

To contact writer get in touch with createspace or send email to nycreativity1@aol.com

Kitty Ditty Little Gaga

For all those who believe in my talent as a writer, a writer of books, musicals and plays. I am a member of the Dramatists Guild and ASCAP.

(A song)

Jay Z, sing it with Lady Gaga.

Maybe Lady Gaga wrote a song
'bout the raining of cats and dogs
without a home
to roam the city.
Pity it's the way it is.

Food for the hungry,
a soft bed.
People adopting you
so you'll be fed.

Jay Z, sing it with Lady Gaga.

Maybe Lady Gaga wrote a song
'bout the raining of cats and dogs
without a home
to roam the city.
Pity it's the way it is.

Food for the hungry,
a soft bed.
People adopting you
so you'll be fed.

Jay Z, sing it with Lady Gaga.

What will follow
is not hollow.
It is my direction
to a special apple
that has a reflection
of a cat on it.
Kind of magical
and as it is shown and glows
a Mrs. Worthington speaks the words
of a story having to do with two cats.
It is quite like the following tale
a cat tale
and I hope to have you on my sail
to embrace it
and face it
whiskers and all
let's have a ball.

**What is ideal for each measure.
I would love this tale to be performed
once more on a stage for all to treasure.
It's a tale about trying to save darlings.
I use a rather small space
but each time the applause keeps building.
One and all
every face,
they love it right away from the start.
I am tempted to call an actor
to play the part
but my show business sense
says I am not dense
about acting – I can do it.
So I have decided to perform it again
and now to find a bigger theater.
Mr. producer, open your door.
There's a lot of feeling in store
for you if you allow me to do
this piece.
I beg of you.
And don't say go to Greece.**

I want a New York stage.
A sign: "stage rental, reasonable."
I'll walk in.
Sir, it's only $50 dolllars?
I'll take it.
I'll make it.
Won't break it.
Some actors there auditioning for a play?
Come in, you'll be entertained.
Won't be pained
Like at your audition.
Thank you for coming.
The show in all its glory.
A wonderful story.

I'll put on this hat with a feather.
A felt hat with more than one feather.
Maybe it's Sicilian.
To me it's worth a million.
Creates character as I speak.
And there will be other hats.
And maybe a puppet of a cat.
Oh how thrilling.
All for the killing.

**I want to believe that one day
all will be well with cats
through good thoughts and action.
No snakes to ruin something,
nothing to sting,
destroy something beautiful,
Evil enemies on the attack,
Get back.
You listening?
Oh but someday soon
you could change
to a new tune
and be kind
and refined.
And have no danger in your eyes,
you'll be one of the good guys.
All will be well with cats.**

Lewis and clark, lead the kitty
to safe places.
Restoreth her soul,
Reviveth her goal,
let her not be a victim
to roll in the mud.
Let no animal attack her,
the ones with big teeth
that keep coming back.
Ugly creatures
with distorted features.
You can't even look at them
because they're so mean
like a thief or crook.

Wouldn't it be good
if they could all change
and be good?
Wouldn't it be good if kitty knows no foxes.
And doesn't have to hide behind some boxes
from some danger out there in the wild
seeking to do harm to them?
Wait.

**Just now kitty is not fearful of things
as it holds on to strings
to play with in starlight of evenings
some magical things.
not thinking of a location
north, south, east or west
certain of this location
that seems to be the best
ah you may have found
your spot in the nation.**

You have your baggage
Yes you've chosen your new resting place.
You sit down in that space
and seem so dignified
though a little broken.
Where is the food? You ask.
you've tried and tried
no luck.
But the man on the truck
throws something to you.
you say thanks,
a dignified cat
with a bowtie and that
velvet vest
like from out west.

Hanging on a twig on a tree
is a clown on a string
you start playing with Mr. clown.
in his urban purple and green attire.
You go higher
still very dignified.
Not ferocious like a raccoon.
A night vision sometimes
who does its own tune, a very brief tune
because he'll soon try to find a forest.
Far far away,
maybe on a carpet ride
but you like this side
with stores and people
and smells of food,
you aint chasing toward a forest.
But you aren't racing toward me yet.

**I whistle a friendly melody
with the words “good night.”
And then a figure will come by
tomorrow in the snow
to try to brush you
and maybe spray perfume
but this time I hear you pleading
for a room
that could be heaven
for you, a dignified cat
called hobo you know
in cat’s row.
You know.**

**Once upon a time
a road somewhere
it's full of mystery
and the moon is watching
and then the sun comes out
and your tune is heard
and I say if Juliet Gaga had a cat
it would be you.
Oh you would really be bringing
the wonder of wonder
that's singing
not growling,
it is really you.**

Your touch,
Your greatness to inspire Gaga
and she would not tire of you
because you are no ordinary cat
though you're found near some garbage,
some bags and things.
You make the sound of a special message
that sings.
Oh how cute
you'd love a garden with fruit
and boxes and trees
and a breeze.
If Juliet Gaga had a cat.

By the way there's a lady on Avenue B
in New York City
who brings many cats to the park.
Hundreds.
then she disappears.
Then a bald eagle appears
Gaga eagle.
He talks and says he's from out west.
He walks and even got an apartment
he said next time she comes by
he'll tell her to work with him
to put up a shelter in the park for the cats
and to really try
to help these innocent babies
and every day to come by with food.

Fools are elsewhere
not with this kind of unusual mood.
Caring hands for the hungry and lonely
in a most brutal time
which is a crime.
Signing off, Gaga eagle.

Yes there was a stray cat.
Furry friend, there you were on a cold lane
needing a song
hoping for no more pain.
You cried "comfort and soothe me."
There you were – beautiful.
I think you smiled.
You were a little wild
but you were not the type to bite.
Oh did I seize that day
a cold January.
Memories to last a lifetime.

Yes there was a stray cat
yes you noticed my kind hand.
It gestured to you to come
and as you came closer I opened the door wide
and more.
I whispered your name "Fritzie."
I asked if someone stepped on thee.
I love thee new feline friend of mine.
You're so fine and kind
and pretty and fluffy.
Maybe from the garden across the street
when you saw me,
felt I had a treat.

Yes there was a stray cat
from Mrs. Wolfram's garden, I think.
I heard your meow saying call me, speak to me.
It was meant to be.
It was so cold the day I found you.
Maybe 40 degrees outside.
"Kitty, kitty, come to me."

You came
shyness and all
you hobbled over
didn't fall.
You were freezing
and still, still very afraid
but you needed someone to be sweet to you
so you came to me.
I prayed it would work out.
And took you to the vet for a checkup.

You know I still call you kitty
even though you're five years old now.
I loved you right away that day
and I think you loved me.
Remember?
Fritzie, we bonded?
You came to me
I could see your nails
but you were so gentle.
You allowed me to pick you up
and cuddle you
whiskers and all.

I took you upstairs
and right into my apartment
and boy were you happy there
running from room to room
and into a closet.
I quickly filled a bowl with water.
You started drinking
then I gave you some food, something soft.
Something you dreamed about
when you were out in the cold
bent, forgotten and feeling old.

Yes there was a stray cat.
You liked every treat.
You liked when I’d comb your hair
to make it neat.
You liked the blanket I gave you
that I put on a chair.
But you liked the bed even more
you wanted to sleep on it.
Take naps on it
And the vet said you were in good health.
Nothing to worry about.

You were so good to me.
so happy
that you found a place,
a home -
no more to roam.
We had a party after a year
and other litte parties
with good food for my dear . . .
then one day you cried.
I was worried.
You'd usually be rolling around
on the ground
or sitting on the window sill.
Now you were so still.

I cried and cried
then one day when i went outside
I found a big cat,
part persian,
so friendly,
so cold outside.
It was part orange and white,
so beautiful.
He kind of resembled Fritzie.

**I opened the front door.
he followed me upstairs
and into my apartment.
a new true friend . . .
I think he was smiling.
When i took him to the vet
I was told he was about three years old.
and I was told he was healthy.
But he had an infection in his eyes
so I was given medication
which I gave him
and his eyes soon got better.
Oh yes . . .
his eyes were yellow
and had a glow.
And soon he would be telling stories
you know, of dragons and monsters
and butterflies would be part of it.
It was a fantasy
made up on the spot
I liked that a lot.**

How did you end up on the street?
Did someone put you there?
In the street.
I wonder about that
if someone could have been so mean to you.
Let's hope no more cats and kittens
are thrown out,
yes thrown out
and end up hungry
and crying their days and nights
and feeding on rats
and getting dirty
and it's dangerous with cars speeding by.
Don't die.

Hero, you are my hero.

**So strong and smart.
Part persian
Part something else.
You only like to eat tuna fish.
That is your wish.
And after eating that
You soon would want to put on a clown hat
and begin to juggle some balls.
You did that.
You were good at it.
You would keep doing it.**

Next there would be a bow in your hair
as you'd go running
from one side of the room to another.
You'd glide by,
seemed like an acrobat.
I took a picture of you
when you did that.
Have many pictures in an album.
I saved all of them.
I raved to people about you
I raved to everyone about you.
I wrote a song about that.
It has a nice melody
and beat
and now another treat.

Yes there was a stray cat
and now another stray cat
Fills my days and nights
with merriment and surprises.
Like the other cat you love to tell stories,
exciting stories
there is art to it
poetry to it
from the start,
even a magical rainbow
like in the Wizard of Oz.
It has a flow to it
as you'd go to your fantasy land
and dream.
Yes it would.
You are a dreamer
in your own special way.

Yesterday, today,
my friend.
From the end of a garbage filled place
with a beautiful face
to enchant me
to sing your sweetest song
to play
in a distinguished way.
Making tonight
like no other night.
Goodnight.
If Juliet Gaga had a cat.

What would you like to eat today?
Liver or chicken?
Or tuna fish?
What is your wish?
Say something to me
in cat tones.

Oh I know, you want some bones
with meat on them
but that's for a dog!
Hero, I have some salmon and cheese.
And some sauce,
I call it a toss thing.
I hope you like it.
I think you said thank you.
And now I'll eat my meal,
vegetables, potatoes, steak.

Oh I'll give you more salmon on your tray,
a feast today.
Love the thought of cats being adopted.
I hope for it and pray
more people to cherish and care for a cat,
I sincerely hope for that.
Politicians , you know where i am at?
Shelters that kill cats must stop the killings.
Politicians, do something about this situation
in this great nation.
Nature, nature, the cat with ten lives.

Mrs. Beaver,
Where are you bringing that cat?
To a shelter?
A kill shelter?
Mrs. Beaver, don't do that,
that poor little cat might die there.
You've had that cat a few years.
has such cute ears
and is so friendly.
How can you toss it out?
There's so much charm to her.
She'd never harm you.

She gave you so much love.
What went wrong
sing a song with her
as she purrs in the song
and you'll see her fur's so beautiful.

Give her a chance
to dance with you
she wants to.

Baby face,
I know you don’t like soda
or pretzels or cookies.

I know you don't like other kinds of food
with a spicy odor.
but when you like it
you lick it down fast, real fast.
It takes just a minute
then you lick your lips,
then soon you're in it,
a drawer in a table.
You squeeze your way in,
I know that you're able
and you sit there a while
next to my papers and things.
You feel like the best of kings.
You deserve it.

Another day
a prayer at the start
a hope for a dream
like in trying to achieve great art

like by monet, the great artist
dreams in the mist

then I think of you
and take your picture.
Did you have to blink?
Oh I just called the painting "cute."
and with some graphics I'll give you a suit.
A real creation for these times,
hip hop chimes.

**Soon after you want me to play with you.
I raise a string up and down
and you play with the string
and again you sing.
Graceful little baby.
I will surely dance with you tonight.
Baby face, you got the cutest face.
I know this is your very special place,
your home,
no more to roam.**

**People out there, give a thought to a cat -
adopting a cat
at the shelter
a thin one or fat,
young one or older
to give the cat a home, your home
to walk around the space
with a beautiful grace
worth a million dollars and more
makes a trillion stars sparkle their glow.**

There you are
so busy from room to room.
or resting near the flowers
that will bloom
or hanging out on the couch.
looking at you for your smile
for a while.

With thank you on its face.
Such kindness in its eyes
and so wise.

Oh to the days when people would flock
to the shelter in town
to adopt a cat
maybe more than one
and the cat inside the cage hissing or
growling would stop that
once outside the cage
and in a home
eating delicious food
at that point one then more cages
would be empty
of a cat or kitty.

Wouldn't that be wonderful
in this city
and others around the world?

Just beautiful
sort of exotic
roman or asian
very symbolic.
A real winner
in every sense of the word.

**As you want and need money
Wall Street or real estate
there is something more than that
something great
a connection with an animal
a frightened animal
to love as you go
into your garden
speaking words "blossoms green
with you a lovely scene."**

**Oh if only there was more kindness
especially toward the weak and cold,
the cat all alone in the world
hobbling around somewhere or in a cage,
it's a story that's old
but needs to be retold
let's help a frightened animal
that's seeking a home,
and wanting to dream
and become whole
with a bit of feline soul.
Very soon I will greet a new friend
for me and my cat
somewhere,
maybe around the bend
from a lot, a deserted lot.
or at the shelter.
See you very soon in this town, my friend.**

**If Juliet Gaga had a cat for a spot,
a royal spot like mine with toys, boxes -
oh I just saw a raccoon from my window.
when the moon comes out,
It's a show of nature's things
passing by.
Even on a desert one early morning
something of nature crawling by
or a big bird doing its routine
in that desert scene.
Wanting something
and enjoying something.
Oh I'm frightened of that raccoon
but he just ran away
to a forest to sway
on some branches
or go up on a hill and disappear.
No more to fear.**

But sometimes there is the not so perfect
city life with - oh I'm frightened –
a little horror there -
maybe a haunted house
or a pirate in the street
oh I'm afraid -
what's happening?

It's only make believe -
there is no haunted house or pirate.
It's an old house, that's it.
And it's Halloween
with that person
in orange a green
saying he's the best dressed pirate
for a Halloween party.
See, just like in storybooks
and each and every fantasy.

And first and especially a toast.

To merriment and food for all,
no hunger large or small,
nothing to worry about,
not stepped on, not feeling poor.
Might be blue birds waltzing
and trees doing a tango
also flowers almost singing.
Nature is in full glory.
It has a feeling of perfection
like nothing is wrong.
What a story.

Suddenly hearing
each beautiful note
that Strauss wrote.

And from me, you know what
I will now sing
loud and clear
for all to hear.

I'm thankful for everything
and love my cat,
my sometimes mischievous cat.
Who knows what he wants?
Yes it's this figure of a clown, Mr. Clown.
See it? He's on the string.
He has beautiful blue eyes -
makes him the guy of all seasons wise.
Kitty is soon playing with the clown.
He's saying funny things to the clown
and even prancing
and dancing.

And now I'll sing a clown song.

Either short or long -
It has graceful notes and goes up, down.
It can be heard uptown.
It's appreciated by young and old
with their beautiful dancing feet.
The figure of a clown moves to the beat.
He's almost alive.
Kitty is purring and moving his tail.
Let's celebrate this in town
my figure of a clown
that my cat loves so much
and it's like he's saying
send me the clown,
my favorite thing in town.

****

I'll send you the clown once more,
I'll do my best
to send you the clown
and the rest . . .

It's always a show of shows
and of course I have a rose
for you, for you
and a word or two.
Send me another cat, dear world
for a fantasy of lights, action and love.
what dreams are made of.

Gaga Eagle, I see you
and that lady from Avenue B
building a shelter for cats in the park.
Oh how pretty
and wise.
Let me help build it.
There's a sign that says enterprise.
Let's hang it near the front door
and feel proud of ourselves.
Each and every buttercup not feeling poor.
Amen.

Love seeks a gaga kitty tonight
remember that –
a chance for a lost kitty,
a dance with kitty
in this city
where cold seems to be
for young and old
braving the winds and
saving up hopes for one last flee.

Pleasure, my friend
is what you stand for
in the little band you play in
with imaginary friends.
A monkey with a grin,
a lion who is tame
in the game,
a fish who you don't eat
but wish to play with,
a scarecrow who is not afraid
and loves to play in the shade.
And an elephant you sit on
and feel you're on a swan

**Also other glorious creatures come
and we all rejoice big time
for the event of event with a rhyme.
To life and to kitty
with majesty in the city.**

Thank you.

A clown with bows and bells
and ribbons and a message
have a good day.
Smile so the day smiles back
and you hold a sack
of toys for others in need
and never forget to feed
your kitty purring again
then hurrying toward you
very gracefully
like a ballet dancer.

Kitty, kitty, once again
your clown smiles some more
as the city does it roar
like a lion sometimes
but the sense of nature
beautiful and calm comes in
like violets in bloom.
Oh how it's in season
As I look outside in my room.

**That's Gretel,
smart and friendly.
She is Gypsy's new friend
and I love her too.**

I found her
in a shelter.
Gretel in a shelter.
Gretel in a shelter.
Now she is in my home
on East 5th Street.

Some day an enchanted day
will come your way
and a rainbow will appear
and the most wonderful feeling
to make you feel good
will be yours
and you'll smile
making those near you smile to,
a sweet smile for a long while.
And you'll notice your cats
smiling with you.

I’m starting to see my cats
reading, yes reading books
to learn.
How did they learn that?
Miracles happen.
And guess what?
They even walk like humans
down to the school
at which time they each become
a mule.
An animal who they think
would love being in a class
more than being on grass.
That’s how they think.

They tell the teacher in charge
they want to start school.
She says yes
and explains the golden rule
to be a good student
to succeed.
That's a beautiful feeling
the mules listen, learn and
get smarter.
They are called Oskar.
Oskar the mules
at a charter school.
I laugh.

**Soon other animals appear.
A goat is the first one.
He's so happy
to go to school.
He laughs a bit
and tries not to spit.
He's kind of cute
and is wearing his new suit.
I like him.**

A rooster appears.

She sings tra la la and has a cradle lullabye.

**A shark wants to learn
says he won't be dangerous.
I'd be frightened of him.**

Sharks behave no rough stuff.

Then a horse appears
and on it is an Indian
who has a bow and arrow
and many books
for the class
and he sits down with the others
to learn too.
He looks old
but everyone says
that's no problem.
They want him to stay in the class
though he is quite old.
They want to learn
what he has been told
by others before him
about music, poems and tales.
a type like him never fails.

One day they decide to take a bus
a huge bus
the size of a block
to go to the zoo
Bronx Zoo
over the Triangle Bridge
and everyone is so happy.
Each brought a sandwich
and a drink
and they're singing on the bus
and having fun.
and then they arrive at the zoo.

They get off the bus
about 50 students
all shapes and sizes
and ages.
They want to go to the cages.
They select which one to go to
and want to be friendly
and want to speak to the animals.
They have lots to say to buddy.

First the bird cages.
Beautiful birds
and oh sweet melody.
Maybe singing something famous
like by Bach
or Mozart.
Those two were so smart.
They knew how to compose
great art.

I love that blue jay
he likes to play
even has a little tambourine
with bells on it
It's both red and green.
The blue jay even talks
and walks
real human
but he likes his birdland.
and his kind of band.

Eagles, parrots, owls.
Look at them
it's like a chorus
and Oskar the mule conducts
the chorus.
Bird music is heard through
Bronx streets
making people dance
and swing and be joyful
it's beautiful.

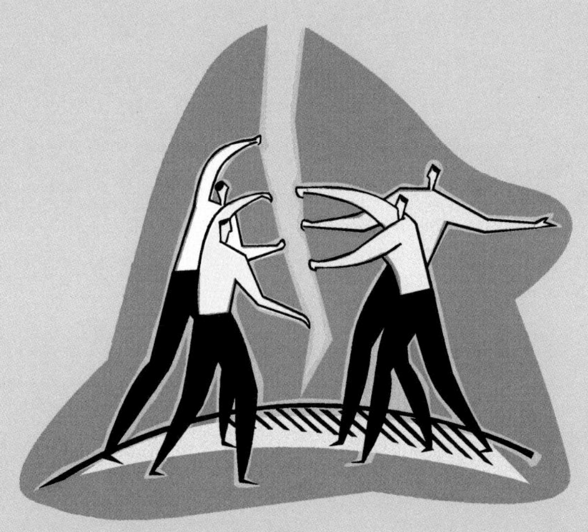

Now to the monkeys
they say hi
where have you been?
They each have a grin
and a rattle and drums
they start playing.
They have a good beat
everyone is swaying
it's a real treat.

One by one we start throwing
them bananas
they're so hungry
they haven't been fed
they eat so fast
they want more and more
till one of them sings
a remarkable melody ,

a piece from an opera
a grand opera
composed by Verdi
a composer from Italy.

I think Toscanini
the famous conductor
came back to life
to conduct the monkeys
on the trees
in their cages
and the bees
humming along
in song.

The elephant walks by
says there's trouble back home.
The students are frightened.
The elephant calms them
urges them to leave the zoo.
The lion wants to help
he is from the nearby cage.
He said he's tame and is allowed
to leave the cage sometimes.
He says he'll follow the bus
as they head back to school.

**A lion who wants to help.
A lion who likes the mules
who will turn back into cats.
Into the bus everyone!
The bus is heading back
to the East Village.
The lion is following the bus,
the long bus.
The lion feels for us
and our plight tonight.
He'll tell us
how to find our way
if we get lost.
We may.
But we pray
and hope to return
to learn.**

Back to the school
the students see signs on it -
school will be closed down.
The cats, my cats are in tears.
They want to have a school.
The teacher also cries.
She'll be without a job.
Other students cry.
Oh my.

**The ghost of Einstein appears,
says not to give up hope.
Einstein, the great scientist.
Also President Lincoln's ghost
trots by.
Says don't give up,
fight those who closed it down.**

**A famous boxer's ghost appears.
Shows some boxing moves
in fighting the enemy
a city agency
that closed down the school.
The boxer says
the school must stay open
for the kids
and the old Indian
and the animals.
But I just heard
the city is taking bids
to sell the building
as soon as possible.
Where will the students go?
Where will they learn?
To know . . .
come, Oskars,
There, you are now cats
you're back home.
Don't worry!!**

Goodnight, hero.
Goodnight, gypsy.
Sleep tight.
Everything will be all right.
We will dance again.
A chance for all kinds of dances.

Good morning.
Here is your beakfast.
Don’t cry.
After breakfast we are
heading off to school.
A big protest is being held
in front of the building.
We’ll march with the others.
We want the school
to remain open.
Learning every bit -
education and wit.
Fun times.
Singing a song,
loving its rhymes.

Now we're near the school
and you are mules again.
And yes they accepted you
no matter how
different you were.
classroom 1a.
A big classroom
like an auditorium.
With high ceilings.
Had fancy woodwork
and designs.
All kinds of lines.
Art in its own way.

TODAY.

Now I'm thinking of great art.
The masters who painted them.
Renoir, Cezanne.
Picasso, Michaelangelo.
Beautiful paintings.
Each a story in itself.
Each to be treasured.
Colorful in a county scene.
Purple, orange and green.

An example of great art.

Trafalgar Square, London, Great Britain

**I celebrate great art.
I long to see great art.
I have a passion for great art.
It moves me.
It relaxes me.
It inspires me.
Let's share it
and care about it
and study it.
Becoming learned
about art -
including theater too
because that's what I do.
Love it!
Plays, musicals.
playing a cd of George Gershwin.
He knew.**

You know, sculpture is precious
tells a deep story of the sculptor
who poured in so much of his soul
with expression -
what an impression -
what eyes, what truth is revealed.
What a strange mood I feel
in looking at you.
Are you real?

**Masterpieces make me tremble -
so perfect
so sure
so daring
so colorful
I am staring.
A remarkable work
yes to believe
every tone coming from it that does achieve
and you want to believe.**

And other works out there
from different centuries.
Glory in them.
A story in them.
Different styles,
Some more colorful, some more gray
Some with flowers.
Some with towers.
Love going to museums to see them.
Guggenheim Museum,
Metropolitan Museum of Art.
Brooklyn Museum,
The list goes on.

Love the paintings
of the stars and the moon
with a bit of tune.
With the sound of strings
and harps.
Nothing that stings.
So special.
I wish the time with a valley,
or mountainside scenery -
be alive to me.
Come alive to me.
I see the most beautiful tree.

Clouds in morning glory.
Enchantment like in a story.
With characters
And poetry.
And reverie
and being merry.
The public school offers that.
Lost art becomes found art.
It's dear to my heart.

Look!
There are beautiful flowers.
Smell the flowers.
Roses and violets.
The horse might drum
and find beats as it goes by
but he won't step on the flowers.
Yes they'll live and bloom
even in winter, no doom.

A fiddler is playing
as nature is saying
it's living and beathing.
Love its purples
no bit of grays
on days like these
and the bees
their hum
seems to please.

**Thinking still of the Bronx Zoo
in winter noon we were
all dreaming
with the animals in cages
dreaming with us
and we seem to be united
and feeling for one another
and ribbons appear on the backs
of some.
It's as if a celebration
would begin.
The time for no problems
in us and none in the world.
Peace.
Amen!**

Remembering again
when we headed back to the city
singing again and again.
A chorus, my friend.

Remembering, still remembering
into the bus
the very long bus
the rooster and shark
the mules, the horse
the Indian
and others.
Back over the bridge
and into manhattan
heading to the east village
finally arriving.
I remember how it really was.
The school was gone.
The bus driver driving
closer and closer
and we saw it was gone
where once we sang
the whole gang.

We are all crying.
What happened?
Was there a storm?
A rough storm?
Strong winds that wouldn't
let go,
you know.
Ocean winds where once
it was calm
and gently blowing
and flowing.

Where did my school go?
Why did this happen.
Old presidents from years back
came and tried to find answers
Lincoln, Roosevelt,
Truman, Kennedy.
They tried hard
for the right words
they mumbled a bit
used wit
seeking the magic words
speaking so nice.
No answers, my friend
seemed like the end.

A special school gone
disappeared
all its memories
seasons of reveries
merriment
through the ages
its pages of history
are no more
its door to truth and wisdom
that I crave for
gone away
today.

I want to learn
so do the others
there's nothing like learning.
The old Indian is crying
he was really trying
to find the magic of life
which in old age seems to go.
He saw in youth the wonder
the mystery
the beauty
of seeking the inner spark
to make things happen
in sunshine, in the dark.
Possibilites -
no enemies.

The grocer, Lopez, on the corner
brought food for everyone.
donuts, no caviar.
pizza, meatballs.
what a shame
a building falls
and slips away.
we try to calm down
us gathered together wondering
what storm and what thundering
caused this.
hold my hand
as I try to understand
the loss of
this building.
it went down
in this town.

I hope there is a school for us
down the avenue or up the hill
or right here.
Something to be built
to end the chill.
Starting with a plan
to rebuild
which is not easy
there has to be money
and the desire to do it
and carry it through.
like a miracle.
Mr. Lopez, thank you for the soup
and sandwiches
and milk for us students
Mr. Lopez, you care a lot.
I care about this lonely spot.

**Soon to bloom
each and every room
books to learn
teachers to teach
and reach out to the students.
A principal who does his job good
like he should.**

**A big piano for music classes.
The music teacher conducting
the chorus.
Sounds of the masters so precious.**

Builder, where are you?
Come in from wherever you are?
From big deals you're doing
make time for us
like a Christmas gift
and do it, renew it.
Let it happen
forget the tower you need.
Start this, lead the construction,
lead.
Design, build.
I hope for this space to be filled.

Square feet
in the millions
for us dancing feet
to dance again.

It will happen.
It must happen.
We mustn't fail.
We have to succeed.
To do math, to read,
to sing
to feel like a king.
Inside the walls
there'll be musical halls.
I hope.
I really hope.

Now we're going home
to be hero and gypsy again
In an apartment on East 5th Street.
Two cats who used to go to school.
Learning the golden rule
as a mule.
Not mermaids, just a mule.
That school's frozen scene
must flower in green.

**A building has to rise
brick by brick
floor by floor
inch by inch.
Using machines
not a stick.
Beams of steel
to support the thing
with a crew of workers
pounding and scraping
and taping.
Big business of building
each and every part
from the start.
To develop this grand scheme,
a dream.**

A dream of a school.

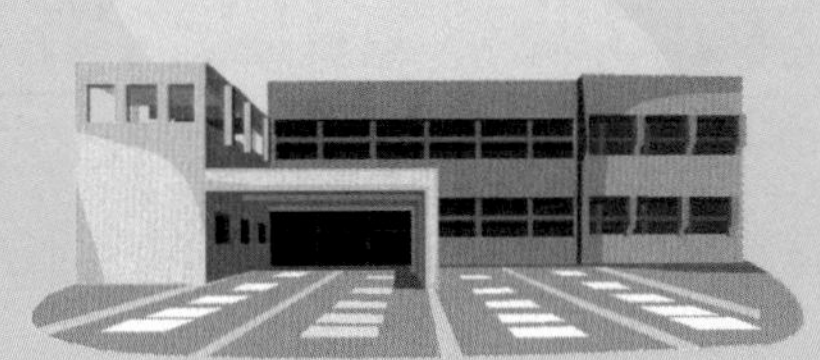

Government says there's trouble
with the budget.
Maybe there'll be higher taxes.
maybe less money to fund this
and buy axes.
Where is the money?

There has to be money.

Come on, Mr. Wall Street.
don’t stop,
don’t embarrass yourself
by any defeat.
don’t be a jackass
and let it pass.

There's a long word -
entrepreneurs -
people with a vision
who have worked on deals
they believe in
no matter how bad.
The government is trembling
They start remembering
old towers
their father built,
the powers he had to do it,
less money never stopped him.
he stayed at it no matter how
slim his finances were.
Daddy and big daddy
were dreamers
in the scheme of things.
Bold and proud
and strong in the money crowd.

No more storms
for two one time stray cats
who want to return to school
soon.
Also for the hundreds of others
with big dreams
and the old Indian on his horse
not ready to say goodbye.

Not ready to say goodbye.
Saddle up,
stranger
ride your horse
to Thomkin's Square
new classes for
young and old
when the school
on East 5th Street
is rebuilt.

**For you,
an old Indian,
for a rooster,
a shark,
two stray cats
and many others
good luck
good night.**

**May real estate
try with all its
might to
carry out
this deal for real.**

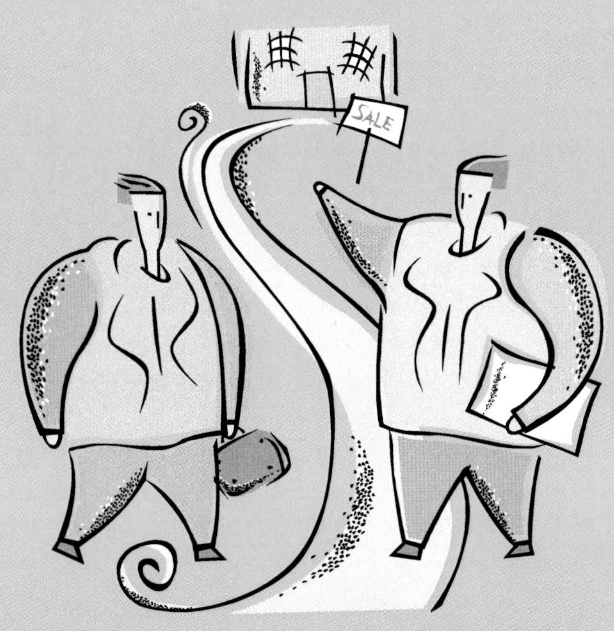

EPILOGUE

There's the cat
Looking, wanting
Like a tramp, a Charlie Chaplin one.
Asking for something,
Asking to sing.
Going up the stairs
Finally to some chairs
And some food of course.
Nature's force
To care and bring love.

Made in the USA
Monee, IL
24 November 2021

82991488R00081